All Was Love

The End

Today was a good day to die

The air was cool and breezy

And it was easy, to fly

Into heaven on a beam of light

Watching others in flight

The clouds disappeared

And so did fears

And all at once,

All Was Love

I looked behind

And in my mind

Was everything I thought I knew

But didn't really know

Until I let it go

And all at once,

All Was Love

God took my spirit

And spread it around

It trickled so far down

It became

a raindrop, a seed, a tree

It became me

God then held my soul

Til it was pure as gold

Kissed me with life again

I whispered Amen

And all at once,

All Was Love

The Beginning

Dedicated to Tammy

All Was Love is dedicated to Tammy, a beautiful spirit whose soul took flight at age 18.

On the day after her transition from this life, due to an automobile accident, Tammy's spirit touched Kristina's spirit and revealed her experience of transition from this world into something more. Tammy passed on what it is to truly feel the connection with everything and everyone. She shared what it means to reside in a state of love, where all fear fades away. As the awakening of Tammy's soul flowed through Kristina, it flowed out from Kristina as words and those words became the poem and the book, *All Was Love.*

To learn more about Tammy's transition and Kristina's life journey, or to order copies of the book, *All Was Love,* for friends and loved ones, please visit www.allwaslove.com.

Kristina Ashley

has been interested in death, dying and grief since she was in her early twenties. She read many books, took classes in college about these interests and had truly powerful experiences with clients doing past life regressions as a certified hypnotherapist. She always felt there was something beyond the physical body and that the soul doesn't die. It retains memory and lives on, building upon its experiences for inner growth and full realization of itself. Kristina has also been in the presence of souls crossing over in her work as a caregiver, affirming to her that the times of birth and death are truly the most powerful of every being. This book is the result of a long personal spiritual journey and her openness to the soul, Tammy, that connected with Kristina while her soul was transitioning through the experience of death. It is Kristina's hope that *All Was Love* will help change the way most people think and feel about death, life and love.

Trea Christopher Grey's lyrical abstract paintings are enjoyed in collections around the world, including New York City, Miami, San Francisco, Dubai and Sedona, AZ, where he resides. There is a playful spontaneity expressed in his paintings and an exuberance of joy and beauty. As a color blind artist, he brings to his work an intuitive wisdom, a vision that expresses the spirit of color. Trea uses unorthodox color choices that bring the riches within worlds to life. His art inspires the imagination and invites a deeper look into the feeling nature of color. There is creative freedom here that goes beyond the conventional. Trea says, "Creating art is an action of love. In a blending of heart, mind and spirit, each painting carries best wishes and intentions for myself and all worlds."

Kimall Christensen's book of knowledge is nature.

Beauty is his guiding light and creativity his abiding joy. In this spirit Kimall held each All Was Love detail with intimate care. His desire was clear; to reflect the beauty and depth of possibility that is at the heart of this creation. Shining throughout All Was Love is Kimall's refined sensibility and creative nature. His talent in graphic design, photography and digital imaging carries Kristina's intentions for the book cover to cover. Kimall has helped to create a special kind of book with Kristina and Trea that give the viewer space to feel connected to inner peace. It was their combined intention to have love flourish on every page, thus Kimall freely shared his heart and steady hand to see the dream of this book unfold.

CONTACT INFORMATION

To order books and read more about the creation of *All Was Love*,
Go to www.allwaslove.com

To contact or see the work of artist, Trea Christopher Grey:
- email: trea@SedonaSkies.com
- www.TreaChristopherGrey.com
- www.WorldsofGoodFortune.com

Magia Publishing
PO Box 3594
Sedona, AZ 86340

ISBN 978-1-4507-8232-6

© 2018 Magia Publishing, All Rights Reserved
This book may not be reproduced in whole or in part without written permission from the publisher, except by a reviewer who may quote brief passages in a review; nor may any part of this book be reproduced, stored in a retrieval system, or transmitted in any form or by any means electric, mechanical, photocopying, or other, without written permission from the publisher.

www.ingramcontent.com/pod-product-compliance
Lightning Source LLC
Chambersburg PA
CBHW041116070526
44584CB00002B/187